# Step Into the

# SPOTLIGHT

11 Inspiring Female Entrepreneurs share stories and strategies on how you too can expand your influence and attract the right customers by stepping into the spotlight.

## Compiled by Colleen Biggs

*CEO & Founder of ColleenBiggs.net,*

*B You B Strong, LLC*

*Colleen Biggs*

Be you Be strong

# Get to Know the 11 Motivated Authors in this Book!

Want more of our authors? I did too! Getting to know the authors and adding the additional benefit to dive deeper into their stories and strategies is available to you anytime, anywhere.

Go to www.StepIntoTheSpotlightResources.com now before you forget. Bookmark the page and forever return for inspiring messages, reminders of how to expand our influence, and consistent practices to apply to your business and life today. For a list of the authors, turn to the table of contents page. Also, on that page are private video interviews with each author, get to know them.

Colleen Biggs, Corporate dropout turned millionaire in 3 years of showing up and stepping into the spotlight in the entrepreneurial world she calls the "Millionaire Playground". Want to learn more about Colleen? Visit her at www.ColleenBiggs.net.

Published by Jumpstart Publishing, PO Box 6, Roseville, CA 95661. (916) 872-4000 www.JumpstartPublishing.net

## DISCLAIMER AND/OR LEGAL NOTICES

While all attempts have been made to verify information provided in this book and its ancillary materials, neither the authors nor publisher assume any responsibility for errors, inaccuracies, or omissions and are not responsible for any financial loss by customer in any manner. Any slights of people or organizations are unintentional. If advice concerning legal, financial, accounting or related matters is needed, the services of a qualified professional should be sought. This book and its associated ancillary materials, including verbal and written training, are not intended for use as a source of legal, financial or accounting advice. You should be aware of the various laws governing business transactions or other business practices in your particular geographical location.

## EARNINGS & INCOME DISCLAIMER

With respect to the reliability, accuracy, timeliness, usefulness, adequacy, completeness, and/or suitability of information provided in this book, Colleen Biggs, B You B Strong LLC., its partners, associates, affiliates, consultants, and/or presenters make no warranties, guarantees, representations, or claims of any kind. Readers' results will vary. Any and all claims or representations as to income earnings are not to be considered as average earnings. This book and all products and services are for educational and informational purposes only. Check with your accountant, attorney or professional advisor before acting on this or any information. Colleen Biggs, B You B Strong LLC., and/or Jumpstart Publishing and its affiliates are not responsible for the success or failure of your business, personal, health or financial decisions relating to any information presented in this book.

Any examples, stories, reference, or case studies are for illustrative purposes only and should not be interpreted as testimonies and/or examples of what readers and/or consumers can generally expect from the information. Any statements, strategies, concepts, techniques, exercises and ideas in the information, materials and/or seminar training offered are simply opinion or experience, and thus should not be misinterpreted as promises, typical results or guarantees (expressed or implied).

ISBN: 978-0-578-93870-7

PRINTED IN THE UNITED STATES OF AMERICA

**"**

*If learning is beneath*
*you, then leadership is*
*beyond you.*

- Colleen Biggs

# Dedication

This book is dedicated to all of those that taught me along the way, mentored, and sponsored me. A special thank you to Ruk Adams and Leo Smart for your belief in me that I could conquer anything I put my mind to.

If it wasn't for God and my husband, Robert Biggs, I wouldn't be the person I am today. Thank you to all of the women in my life and all of the community members. Surrounding myself with people that fuel my fire, challenging me to show up as me everywhere, every time, and continuously urging me to persevere is the key to happiness and extreme success.

This book is for you that has Gisele-like intensity to make it happen. If you desire to step into the spotlight and do so without asking the permission of others, this book will inspire you to be more, do more, and have more!

# Praise for
# *Step Into the Spotlight*

## Your Network is Your Net Worth

*"The truth is that if you are hiding behind your fear, Colleen Biggs will tell you straight up that she was a corporate dropout until she realized hiding won't get you success, and FEAR will only hold you back.* **Colleen has helped women across the globe by helping them to "Step Into the Spotlight to Expand your Influence."** *- Shea Vaughn* Founder / CEO WorldWide TV / WWTVN / www.worldwidetv.tv Creator / CEO SheaNetics® / SheaVaughn.com SAG-AFTRA / Producer Creator / CEO SheaNetics® | Actress

*"Colleen Biggs has created a world where you can step up and into your spotlight with confidence. She lives this mantra by providing experiences, creating opportunities, and supporting women to become their best selves.* **This book provides valuable insights on how**

*women can get out of their own way and succeed. I highly recommend it as your next read." - Debi Corrie, CEO of DebiCorrie.com*

*"Colleen Biggs is the CHAMPION for all women. She is a woman with a huge personality and heart that is even bigger. She sees women for who they are, what they can do, who they can become, and she offers them the opportunity to see themselves as she does. Sometimes all it takes for a woman to move mountains is to stand behind and see another woman who is doing it. Colleen is doing it!" - Jean Kuhn, CEO of JeanKuhn.com*

*"Every word that Colleen wrote in this book is worth reading.* **She has the right strategy and honesty to lead entrepreneurs to the top.** *I have personally known her to be the real deal. Authentic, smart, and accomplished. Her superpower is that she is a true connector and in business, building the right relationships is of utmost importance." -* Didi Wong International Award-Winning Keynote Speaker, Hollywood Film & TV Producer & Financier, Speaking Coach, Angel Investor & UN Goodwill Ambassador

# Table of Contents

**66**

# Our only limitations are those we set up in our own minds.

- Napoleon Hill

**99**

**Colleen Biggs**

# Introduction

Do you want to be seen, be heard, and be visible? Do you want to gain authority, own your future, and nurture relationships in your community?

*Step Into the Spotlight*, is for women who have this burning desire within them to make an impact on the world. This book is dedicated to female entrepreneurs that knows she has a purpose and wants to have greater exposure to reach more people.

I assisted over 340 businesses to open their doors and realize massive success over the last 20 years. Within that period, I was able to discover the secret ingredient to success: EXPOSURE. It wasn't until just over 2 years ago, that I dropped out of corporate and started 3 businesses of my own that I put all of those practices that I taught for 20 years to work. And guess what, it worked! I have become a millionaire and so can you! *Step Into the Spotlight,* is written for the new entrepreneur, the seasoned entrepreneur, and the purposeful driven female entrepreneur that desires to have more out of her business to create more opportunities in her life.

This is the first volume of the book, *Step Into the Spotlight,* and will certainly not be the last. This volume charters into the territories of the real-life experiences of several experts that have found themselves without a voice at one time or another in their lives. We all suffer imposter syndrome at every level and the authors in this book explain how they were able to overcome those setbacks and *Step Into the Spotlight* even when they didn't know that they deserved it or would be able to withstand the pressure.

The authors with whom I have collaborated on this book are experts in their industries and in what they teach. Our goal with this book is to provide you with the inspiration of their stories as well as practical/tactical tips you need to stop playing small, reduce your shrinking and *Step Into the Spotlight* where you belong.

These are the areas that we cover in the *Step Into the Spotlight* book and we urge you to identify with the areas you need the most assistance on and take advantage of all of the freebies that our authors are providing for you to get to know them.

Who we surround ourselves with becomes our net worth! Remember your network is your net worth. Find the tribe and place the people directly in your life that fuel your success, not suck the energy from all of your ideas. They're out there and our authors are a good place to start for forming your tribe. They want to hear from you and so do I!

If you enjoy one or more of the chapters in this book, we urge you to reach out to the author(s). You will find in-depth interviews with each of the authors here www.StepIntoTheSpotlightResources.com. The authors want to hear from you. Let them know that they inspired you, motivated you, or encouraged you to *Step Into the Spotlight*. They also want to know how they can assist you in your growth in all of the areas that this book covers.

If you are looking for more information on how you too can join the Leap community to expand your exposure or how you can get in touch with me directly to assist you in reaching your peak performance as an entrepreneur, reach out to me at: www.ColleenBiggs.net.

## Allison Lewis

# Create Who You Want to Become

Being creative was never part of my persona, for the first 20 years or more of my life. I came from a conventional family like many of you. A dad and mom who worked hard to meet our family's needs, including me and my two older brothers. Thus, I grew up following the norm: go to school, do good, get into college, graduate, and find a job. You know the basics. This meant creativity was never a high priority.

I went through the motions like a good little girl; graduated from college and started work right after. One day, I realized that I was doing the same job for ten years already. I also realized how monotonous and less of a challenge my work had become. I felt like I wasn't using my gifts and talents (even though I didn't know what those were yet). Don't get me wrong, I appreciated the job, all it had to offer, and everything that I learned. I am a believer of soaking up and absorbing all you can from your current situation because you never know when it is going to be of use to you in the future.

So, since I was bored, unmotivated and in a rut… I set out to make a change. I set out to find something more. I set out to create who and what I wanted to become.

Entrepreneurship wasn't really on my radar either, it was right up there with creativity. At one point, I kept seeing it all over the web. I was intrigued when I saw lots of bloggers and influencers popping up all over social media. Not sure what these terms really meant, or anything about the people who were creating content for these blogs and social media, I followed them anyway….and eventually, on a whim, I started my blog *Absolutely Alli*. Not knowing where it would take me, it turned out to be the best decision of my life. Unaware of it then, my blog would take me on a journey of self-discovery, exploration of creativity, and entrepreneurship by planting the seeds for my business Absolutely Social.

Although a challenge in the beginning, I grew my social media presence, as an influencer, from 0 to over 100k collectively throughout all my platforms combined. As I dove into blogging and influencing, I made it my business to learn the strategies, the dos and don'ts, and most importantly how to monetize my social media. As I grew into this role of influencer, others started noticing me and asking for advice regarding social media, influencing, and content creation. This ignited a passion within me to not just become an influencer, but to support other entrepreneurs reach their full potential on social media by helping them in their businesses.

Regardless if they are a blogger, a boutique owner, trying to amplify their brick-and-mortar store visually, or starting a career in social selling, I help amplify their own influence online. This prompted me to start my business Absolutely Social, which has digital courses, books, social media management, and influencer coaching to help others accelerate their social profiles.

After I started my blog, I realized creativity was essential, not only for the life I wanted to live but also to be a successful entrepreneur. Creativity is essential to step into the spotlight to share your gifts and talents.

So how do you do that...?

There are 3 key components that you need to focus on in order to step into the spotlight and create who you want to become.

**First, You Need to Feed into Yourself**

Just like you nourish your body with food, you must nourish your mind for your entrepreneur journey. Feeding into yourself could be the difference in being in the spotlight or being behind the scenes.

**Steps to Feed into Yourself:**

1. **Create a business plan or a plan of action for your business.** This plan should include your mission and core values, social media and branding strategies, making sure you know your avatar or customer/client composition. While creating this plan ask yourself questions like: what need does this product or service

fill? Are there any other products or services like this on the market? If so, how does mine differ? Also, in your plan explore your financials (how much money do you need to make? How many relationships do you need to foster in order to meet your financial goals?).

2. **Invest in yourself.** Take time out to continually learn more. Those who get comfortable, never really grow. Attend conferences, read books, invest in a coach, outsource things you don't want to do or can't do. Partner with people who can help group your business.

3. **Find a mentor who can guide you on your entrepreneurial journey.** You might even have multiple mentors. Look for one that has the accomplishments that you are striving for, someone that can help you with your business plan and can introduce you to other people in that circle.

4. **Network.** Go to events and conferences that are centered on your business or have like-minded people. I have always heard you never want to be the smartest person in the room, so make sure you are engaging and associating with others that up level you. This also

means spending limited time with people that don't work to help you accomplish your goals.

These steps will set you up for creating a better and stronger you!

## Second, You Need to Be Heard

We have all heard that the most successful person is not the one who talks the most or spends the most money. It is the one who is most recognized. I had an ex-coworker once say to me "I see you everywhere", she didn't mean she physically saw me, but she saw my brand and face everywhere. And that is what you are trying to do-- to be heard.

Basically, you need to be the most creative. In order to be heard you must put yourself out there, you must show up, you yourself and your brand must be recognized. Start volunteering your services for nonprofit organizations, book yourself for free speaking engagements, amp up your social media by coming up with a plan (or getting a social media manager like me!) and ask past customers for testimonials you can share.

If you are not using every single opportunity to educate people on what you do or what you have to offer, then you might miss an opportunity to work with future clients or customers. Being heard can be accomplished in a multitude of ways. Use as many as you can so the next time someone you know sees you, they will say "I see you everywhere", and then you won't have to explain what you do because they already know.

## And Third, You Need to Monetize You

In business and social media, the big buzzword is monetization. It means how your business makes you money online. I think one thing that many people forget is that you are your brand, not just the name and products you attach to it. Monetizing you is more than just about making money, it is about you, yourself and the way you carry yourself as a person. You must hold yourself to a higher standard, as a person, because you are representing a brand. You literally are a walking/taking billboard for your brand, clients, and products you offer.

If you are not living the part, how do you expect someone else to want to buy into it? The life you actually live has to be authentic to you and your brand. No telling people to do one thing and you doing another. To monetize your brand, you must monetize you first. You have to live the lifestyle that someone else wants their brand to be associated with. If your brand is to help people run their first 5K, and you put on your personal social media how much you dislike running or that you have never ran a 5K before. Do you think that people are going to buy your services? No, of course not.

Creating who you want to become is more than just dreaming up a life as a business owner. It takes dedication and you must always be feeding into yourself so that you can evolve. Stepping into the spotlight and coming into your own will allow you to be heard and help others along the way.

If you would like to learn more about monetizing and maximizing your social media for business, sign up for my newsletter at www.AbsolutelyAlli.com, and if you want to take a deeper dive into social media influencing check out my book and masterclass: *The Business of Blogging and Social Media Influencing*. You can also follow me on social media by searching @absolutely_alli or @absolutely___social.

# About Allison Lewis

Allison is the blogger, influencer and content creator of Absolutely Alli. After years of working in this space, she discovered her passion for helping others build their digital brand. Allison then started her company Absolutely Social, which provides social media management, consulting and digital strategy. Cultivating digital lifestyles, she is the go-to expert in blogging, influencing, and content creation, which empowers women and businesses to show up online and monetize their message.

## Carey Conley

# Your Vision, Your Guide

When I was in my mid-twenties, I was doing what most of us were taught; get a degree, get married, and get a secure job where you can work your way up the ranks. My husband, Ross, and all of our friends seemed to be doing this happily. I was changing jobs every two years because I thought I couldn't find the right career.

At one of those jobs, I met a woman who would become my first mentor, and she said something so profound that it changed my life. It brought me to where I am today over 30 years later. She told me that I could create my life to look however I wanted. I just needed to get crystal clear on what that looked like and get that vision in writing.

So, I took a day off of work, and on a legal pad of paper, I wrote in great detail what my dream life would look like. I was taking what most people do with making a vision board to a much deeper level. It went beyond just envisioning the 'things' I wanted. It was mainly about the kind of person I wanted to be for myself, my family, and for the people I wanted to impact. Without knowing it then like I do now, I was aligning with my purpose, which would become my compass and anchor for my life and what was to come.

About three years later, after writing that big, bold vision, I became a mom. I was introduced to the beginning of my entrepreneurial path and stepped into the network marketing industry to work from home while raising my kids. Being at home with my kids was a big part of my vision, so it was an easy decision to make but not one without challenges. You may already know this, but part of being successful in that industry is the personal growth you must go through while recruiting and growing a team. I believe it is the number one factor why most people fail. For people to join you, they must first believe in you. It is challenging because most of us (if we are honest) struggle with self-doubt and belief in ourselves.

My vision for my family got me through all those challenging times. I hit a LOT of walls. My best friend who recruited me died suddenly a year after we started. My husband was not a fan of me doing the business, which strained our marriage. Family and friends thought I was crazy. And I had multiple team members quit.

What kept me going was simply this, and I have come to believe this is the secret to getting through adversity: What you envision MUST BE BIGGER than the walls!

The way you get through anything is by wanting something more than where you are now. I didn't drift when all of those things happened because my vision kept me anchored in persevering. I made it to the top rank in the company while raising my children. I earned many things; most importantly, I was becoming the person I had envisioned. I felt then I had won the ultimate prize in life.

When our children went off to college, I decided to expand on another desire. I wanted to help more people write their visions on paper so they could follow their true purpose. I had been teaching my team for years to do this and loved that part of my role! I had created and conducted many leadership workshops for them. I got so much encouragement from everyone on how much it helped them, it genuinely validated my desire to become a speaker and coach on a bigger scale. The twenty years of growing that business was really about getting groomed and prepared to step into a new spotlight.

I began by doing small vision workshops, which then turned into hosting bigger events, leading people into small group coaching sessions. From that experience, I was getting very comfortable with public speaking and learned that this was my true passion.

Unfortunately, I didn't know what was just about to happen...two years after launching this career and the day after signing on to partner up with another coach to start mentoring entrepreneurs; my husband took his life. Our beautiful family of four was now reduced to the kids and me.

Cole had just graduated from college. He accepted a job to start in one month in another state. Our daughter, Laurel, started her junior year at a university also in another state. To say this changed my life forever would be an understatement. All the plans for our family's future the way I saw it was gone.

The whirlwind began. After a month of getting through the memorial service, being with family and friends, and working through the beginnings of the grief and shock, we had to make some decisions. I got Cole moved so he could start his new job, and I started living part-time in two states. I had new clients who were ready to get started, and my daughter also needed to get back to school. There was very little time to grieve, and I had to keep our family together as much as possible.

Three short years later, the second catastrophic event of my life occurred. We lost Cole to suicide. I can't form any words for you to define my feelings and what that did to me on so many levels. Losing Ross was hard enough, but losing a child is truly indescribable.

I took some time off for the next year to get through this with Laurel. We stayed close together for many months, and I only did what I was already committed to doing. A few short months later, she got engaged and married a year after.

The biggest question people have asked me is, 'how in the world are you still functioning?' My answer is this: my vision of who I am and what I am called to do from here got bigger. My vision and my faith became my lifeline— my anchor in those storms.

As you can imagine, these tragedies also put Laurel and me in a whole new spotlight. We have been very open about our lives, and we decided to write a book entitled *Keep Looking Up*. We launched the book on 11/11/19, which would have been Cole's 27th birthday. We went on a small book tour (Laurel, now pregnant with her son), and started speaking together. We are both very clear that people need vision and they need to know their purpose now more than ever. We felt Ross and Cole working through us to accomplish this mission.

Although this would not be how I would choose to be in the spotlight, I can now look back and see how everything I have gone through has helped me become the person I asked to be and how I am being used to help others. Without all of the lessons and life challenges, I could not have handled where I am now and going next.

If you resist writing your vision and following your true purpose, I want to encourage you today. You DO have a mission to carry out, and you are here to make this world a better place. I know you can feel that. And, if you are waiting for the 'right time' or for the fear to go away, you will be waiting forever. Most people die with regret simply because they don't take the most crucial step: to take the time to get clear on your deepest desires. If you are thinking about it, you are equipped to do it! And I promise you that if you are dreaming it, God's got the plan and has your back!

Here is one last tip I want to give you to find the courage to take that step and begin: You have to make it about something bigger than you. People with low self-esteem tend to get discouraged and give up easily on themselves. My vision has always been attached to becoming better for my family and now the people I serve. On the days you feel like you can't do it, look at those faces and know they need you right now to find their courage to follow their purpose too.

**I have a free download for you that I want to give to you as a present, it's my *Vision is Victory Workbook*! Get access to that, and my Vision Driven Life Facebook group, a one-on-one call with me and learn more about our Vision is Victory Academy too, all online at:**

**www.CareyConley.com/SpotlightResources.**

Follow your vision and watch what an impact you can make!

# About Carey Conley

Carey Conley is dedicated to helping you identify your dreams and goals through Vision building and to achieve those goals through discovering your Purpose. She believes that success in life is about following your true passion and knowing what impact you are here to make in the world. Carey draws from more than 2 decades of experience in growing two businesses, decades of being a wife and mom, and her personal journey of life tragedies that she shares with her audience. She not only can relate to her audience why having a clear vision and purpose is the bottom line to professional success but how it becomes the anchor in all the storms of life. It is through her joy and pain, through her success and struggles, that she offers you the greatest opportunity to create a clear path to your destiny by living in your Purpose.

**Colleen Biggs**

# Be Seen, Be Heard, Be Visible

Are you ready to step into the spotlight in your business? You do know the more that you do, the bigger your influence will grow and so will your bank account, right? Staying in the shadows or laying low will only make life pass you by.

I am Colleen Biggs. I am a corporate dropout-by choice. I currently pioneer the way for women by providing them their most sought-after marketing strategy, VISIBILITY!

I have launched over 340 businesses in the last 18 years. I have dabbled in commercial real estate, designed brick and mortar stores, relocated corporate offices, and served on boards that provided camps for girls. I host an elite podcast. I am also an international speaker, and author of three books that have become a #1 Bestseller on Amazon. I'm a high-level consultant and coach, and a ringmaster to 7 kids and 11 grandchildren. I coordinate masterminds for women to travel around the world. All of that to help myself and others collaborate to foster consistent growth to move from success to significance. Whew! That's a lot, right? You better believe it: my life is FULL and I love it!

So, let me ask you a question: Why do you think I shared all of this with you right off the bat?

Because no one is sharing this information about me, it's MY responsibility to share all of my accomplishments, shout from the mountain tops, and put myself in the spotlight, period!

**Research shows that unless you promote and market yourself, you have an 80% chance of failing in your career and in your business in the first 3 years of a start-up!** When was the last time you told others about your accomplishments, who you are, what you do, hobbies you enjoy, or what problem you can solve for them? If you didn't answer in the past 24 hours, then you are not standing in the spotlight, and trust me when I say opportunities are everywhere!

Somewhere along the way, between the age of two and our teenage years, we lost the ability to do whatever we wanted without caring who saw. Like my grandson who loves to throw his sippy cup across the room because he didn't want it anymore, or my granddaughter who walks around half-naked pushing her belly out. Or, any of us who used to ask for exactly what we wanted.

Why do you think that is?

**Society and culture have molded us.** Women, especially, are molded into being in service of others first, instead of asking for what we want or promoting ourselves first as entrepreneurs. In my day, self-promotion was labeled selfish! If you feel selfish for self-promoting, then **you need to hear this.**

The most common answer I get regarding why women don't step into the spotlight is FEAR. Let's break down F.E.A.R.

*The definition of FEAR is to be afraid of (someone or something) as likely to be dangerous, painful, or threatening.*

In my world, FEAR means the "False Evidence Appearing Real" or "Face Everything And Rise". You see, FEAR is not FAILURE or something we should shy away from. Fear is our anticipation and urge to expand and grow, to face everything and rise above, and to face fears head-on, no matter what.

For example, the worst thing that could happen would be:

1. I didn't get the job
2. The client chose not to work with me
3. I didn't convert any of the attendees to my coaching program
4. That marketing strategy didn't work

Looking at all the possibilities that could go wrong, still provides you perspective and understanding of what works, what doesn't, and which path to take. You see, in the end, **taking a LEAP of faith and charging forward with courage, bravery, and confidence, using FEAR as your fuel will always create growth, no matter how small, you still improve and move forward.**

**It doesn't matter what they think because it's not about you anyhow!** Have you heard that phrase? Well, it's true.

What others think about you is in fact their self-reflection. You are the only you that has ever been and the only you that will ever be, so it is up to you to show up in this world exactly as you are, that's it. **No one is looking for the perfect you, they just want YOU!** Now isn't that refreshing?

Wait, did the FEAR just pop back up for you? If so, read above one more time! That's right, it doesn't matter what others think, and fear will always fuel you forward.

So now that you are fueled by F.E.A.R. and not paying attention to what others are saying about you, what's next? How do you successfully step into the spotlight?

I have created a list of **7 Spotlights that are available for everyone**, everywhere to participate in to expand your influence and attract more clients.

1. **Magazine Articles & Blogs:** So many affiliations, including Lead Up for Women, are looking for contributors to write articles, or submit blogs for their websites and digital assets. Do some research and apply to be a contributor. Hint: You can submit the same article

over and over to several different publications to make this seamless and simple.

2. **Virtual & In-Person Networking:** This has, by far, the most return on investment of time. You can meet new people, share who you are and what your purpose is in life, chat with others that are not in your current circle or community, and truly expand your influence. But remember the return is in the follow-up. You MUST nurture these contacts and truly, purposefully connect with them.

3. **Podcasts:** Everyone has a podcast today. There are websites that you can apply to be a guest on a podcast such as Podmatch.com and matchmaker.fm. These are just two examples of hundreds of sites you can apply for being a guest or start your own podcast!! This is the "One to Many" approach. One event, reach hundreds if not thousands. This is a brilliant way to step into your own spotlight to expand your influence.

4. **Live Videos:** People do business with those they know, like, and trust! Build that trust through popping onto daily

Facebook Live's, YouTube, LinkedIn, Instagram Reels, Stories, and more.

5. **Workshops & Seminars:** Create a workshop, 5-Day Challenge, or a One-Day event, and invite others, for free if you would like, to come to join you and teach them your genius! Share how you can solve the problem they are experiencing and how uniquely you can do that for them. Remember, you are extremely unique, so no matter how many chiropractors there are in the world, for example, you have your special way of assisting the healing of your patients and those are the clients you will attract. Like attracts like, so who is your ideal client?

6. **Publicity:** Are you aware you could be a guest on your local, or even a national Television show? It's relatively easy these days to be featured in the media, you just have to be confident in your abilities and ask! Yes, reach out and ask. The media is constantly on the lookout for interesting, inspiring, and motivating stories and guests all the time as well as news.

7. **Clubhouse:** This brand-new online platform allows you to hop into a room and listen to experts, become an

expert and speak to others. You can also create your own room and command authority, share your knowledge, and invite others to join your community.

These are just a few of the ways that you can get the visibility you need to grow your businesses in this oversaturated social media culture we live in today! Back in my corporate days, I played with the notion that there was no "I" in "TEAM". Remember that? Well, if there is no spotlight for me, then how do I get promoted? I didn't! Not until I stepped into the spotlight, stood there, and shouted, *"Hey, look at me, look what I have accomplished, and what I want out of my career"* did I get anyone's attention. It worked! I was promoted 3 times in 5 years before I dropped out from the corporate world. That was the exact moment that drove me to create my organization, Lead Up for Women.

Today, I serve women around the globe by providing them *spotlights* to step into to expand their influence and attract more clients. There is no other day like today. Tomorrow is not promised, and today will turn into yesterday. **We MUST act now to promote ourselves, fueled by F.E.A.R., selfishly to impact the lives of others and by ASKING for what we want.** If your purpose is driven by your desire to make an impact on others, which is 99% of the driving force behind what everyone does, then you must give yourself the permission to push the gas pedal and step into the spotlight, stand there past the uncomfortable moment, and shine! You won't regret it, and neither will we. Because without you, the world is missing out on what you bring to this earth, YOU!

**I invite you to take the next step with me to take your business to the next level. I've created a special page just for those of you reading this chapter and on it there's an opportunity to print a list of Spotlights I recommend,** learn more about Lead Up for Women, attend a Lunch-n-Learn on me, and sign up for a free 30-minute Visibility Strategy Session. In addition, you can check out our Free Digital Magazine and learn how you can be featured IN IT! **Go to: www.StepIntotheSpotlightResources.com now and I'll see you in the Spotlight!**

# About Colleen Biggs

Colleen Biggs is an Award-Winning Peak Performance Consultant with over 20 years of experience, launched over 340 businesses, is an International Speaker, Author, the CEO of three businesses including Lead Up for Women, a community that boasts tens of thousands of female entrepreneurs driven by their passions, support and promote others with a purpose to fuel female voices with power that are leading the way for all women worldwide to dominate the entrepreneurial market.

## Dannella Burnett

# Monetizing Your Message from Stage

The call to speak has been shouted from the rooftops, shared in workshops and discussed in coaching sessions for years, and has only gotten louder. In March of 2019 there were an estimated 40,000 professional speakers in the United States alone and they were generating 1.9 Billion dollars in annual revenue. Income generated by speaking fees as well as books, courses, programs, products and coaching services. As the industry has grown, more and more business owners, coaches and marketers have entered into the speaking world and were stepping onto these stages to share messages of business, health and wellness, relationships, money making and more.

But even with all those speakers there were still more opportunities that remained unfilled.

Before March of 2020, it was estimated that there were more than 7,000 speaking opportunities EVERY DAY in the United States. From smaller networking events or company workshops to larger conferences and expos to corporate trainings, non-profit fundraisers, and more. With all the changes that have taken place, events and speaking opportunities have gone virtual. It might be a setback for some, but, it is estimated to have grown exponentially by eight to 10 times. There is always an abundance of speaking opportunities. However, many speakers still struggle to get on stage and share their messages of inspiration, education, motivation, monetization or transformation. Many struggle with the speed of events and speaking opportunities now in the virtual world.

As an event producer for the last 30 years who advanced to producing national events for the last eight years, my team and I help connect many high-level and high-income-earning speakers to lucrative speaking opportunities. We perform in-depth research and preparation aiming to foster a win-win-win opportunity for the event host, the speaker, and the attendees, respectively. When speakers are in the right environment with the right audience, proper mindset, and good self-perception…magic happens.

Getting visibility and sharing your message is important, however, too many speakers focus on their passion and forget that profit is key to sustainability of that message! Speakers can be so passionate about their message, have a huge desire to serve, help others overcome, want to change the world, but they forget that speaking is a business and there has to be a strategy to make money so the message can grow and the speaker can keep speaking! Messages without monetization go mute!

There are three main pathways for getting paid to speak and a few options within each path. All are great options and viable. All have their own unique challenges and benefits.

**4 Keys to maximize each pathway or opportunity are:**

1. Knowing your strengths
2. Being prepared and positioned
3. Outlining your goals

4. Applying the right strategies

Speakers need to speak, but they also need to get paid. That payment can come before, during or after the talk however, all are viable options.

**The first pathway of speaking is keynote or paid speaking.**

Paid speaking is good for a motivational, inspirational or educational speaker. There is often an application process and the challenge is to show the value not only for the audience, but for the entity that is writing the check. Frequently this would be a corporation, university, non-profit, organization or association that may be hiring a keynote speaker for an annual conference, workshop or other event for their members or employees.

This type of speaking definitely has the most competition and the payoff is getting the payment for the talk, or you may be able to negotiate books sales into the deal but frequently you are not able to promote the rest of your business such as courses or coaching. Showing the tangible value you bring to the audience is often the deciding factor in getting this type of speaking opportunity and negotiating a good rate for speaking.

Attaining impressive testimonials and landing referrals are two very important results to achieve from this path. Having a great speaker one-sheet, or also known as a speaker resume, is also crucial to booking more speaker gigs.

**The second pathway for speaking is paying to speak or sponsorship speaking.**

With your typical "pay-to-play" speaking opportunity, the speaker pays for the opportunity to speak. For some speakers starting out this may seem counterintuitive, but many seasoned speakers prefer this speaking pathway. While you need to be able to discern the right sponsorships for you, this can be the fastest path to growing your list, selling from the stage, filling your business courses and programs and can be far more profitable than getting paid.

Sponsorships can range from a few hundred dollars to tens of thousands of dollars, so understanding how you will use that speaking opportunity to increase conversion is critical. Asking questions about the event host and understanding the audience, the opportunity, the role of the speaker in the event, the other speakers, and the history of the event are all important aspects to consider. Also, it is important to have a contract and clear rules about who is responsible for what especially if something goes awry or doesn't meet expectations. I often prefer this type of opportunity as you are buying the time and the opportunity and frequently can turn this into a big wins financially and for building authority.

**The third pathway is free speaking opportunities.**

In this case, no money changes hands, but there may be a requirement to promote the event, a swap of speaking opportunities or similar trade of value. This can be the best option for gathering contacts, scheduling follow-up consulting or coaching calls and getting exposure to new audiences. With free speaking opportunities, the speaker often offers a complimentary consultation or strategy call, eBook, assessment or content in exchange for the audience's contact information.

This type of speaking has exploded in the virtual world since it opened incredible opportunities to gain visibility, new connections and influence in their industries for many speakers. Keynotes, on the other hand, have been a harder pathway to get consistent and profitable speaking opportunities as more corporate and organizational events have remained postponed or harder to locate as decision makers are working from home and may not be creating as many opportunities for paid speaking gigs.

Sponsorships continue to be a viable option as long as the speaker does due diligence on the audience, the opportunity and the ability to get a return on their investment.

Another great option for speaker visibility that we often take for granted but can similarly impact target audiences are podcasts, social media lives and social media interviews, radio or livestream TV. These interviews are really good opportunities for speakers as they are frequently a free opportunity and can gain great exposure and new connections.

Up to this point I've highlighted ways for speakers to gain visibility by leveraging other platforms – events, summits, podcasts and more created by others and allowing a speaker to share with many and grow their audience, connections and business. It's also a great environment for speakers to create their own platform for exposure.

Virtual events are more economical to produce without the expenses of venue and hospitality. It is also easier to invite larger and more diverse audiences. There may be more needs in the areas of technology and team, but overall, it's still easier to launch an event, podcast or social media "program" than ever.

As we move further into the virtual world and experiment with hybrid events and eventually seeing more in person stages come back to the forefront, it will be interesting. We will continue to support speakers and event clients by getting the visibility and monetization needed to grow their businesses and make an impact. By understanding the needs of events, of speakers and of audiences, I'm confident the best opportunities will continue to present themselves for our clients and our own business.

**To best be prepared, positioned and ready to be profitable, I invite to go over to**

**www.SpeakersNeedtoSpeak.com/spotlight**
**and grab the free CRUSH IT FROM THE STAGE CHECKLIST!** With this comprehensive checklist you'll be prepared to step into the spotlight and maximize your money and your message.

# About Dannella Burnett

Owner of Encore Elite Events & Speakers Need to Speak, Dannella Burnett is a creative force with a passion for connecting experts to those they serve through speaking & events while generating profitable and impactful visibility! Through her connections, millions of dollars have been generated and tens of thousands of lives impacted through speaking and live events! She believes in multiple streams of income, collaboration, and always finding the win-win-win combination!

**Emily Harman**

# Putting Yourself First

Have you ever felt like your dreams were buried under a mound of responsibilities and that somehow you lost yourself along the way? I've been there!

I decided at age 17 to attend the U.S. Naval Academy which ended up determining the course of 38 years of my life. In retrospect, I'm not sure that decision was based on *MY* inner truth.

For the longest time, I felt the need to please others and became a chameleon— adapting and acting the way I felt was expected of me. At work, I was a confident over achiever. But my personal life was a different story. I married a verbally abusive man whom I didn't have the courage to leave, until I realized that the abuse was extending to my children.

As a single parent, I focused on achieving, moving ahead, yet, I **never felt good enough** no matter how much I accomplished. I even remarried (and re-divorced), without recognizing that chameleon Emily was the one making the calls, and the real me was nowhere to be seen.

In 2014, five years prior to my retirement eligibility date, a friend invited me to the World Domination Summit focused on how to live a remarkable life in a conventional world. It planted an idea to create a life that I love, but, ironically I didn't act right away. It took three years, a promotion, and a deep sense of unfulfillment to finally decide it was time to let go.

Fast forward to 2018. I was riding the metro to my job at the Pentagon. I saw crowds of people, eyes down, ear pods in, blank expressions on their faces. I caught a glimpse of my reflection in the train window and realized I looked like that too! I felt suffocated. I was tired of my hectic routine and finally ready to create a life on my terms. *Who am I? What do I want?* I didn't even know.

But as I retired in 2019 and was about to design a new life on my terms, my children's father was diagnosed with cancer, became paralyzed in both arms, and ended up losing his battle within six months of my retirement. During that time, once again, I put everything on hold for my children. I helped care for their father, served as executor of the estate and, worked through a rollercoaster of emotions.

Finally, I decided it was time for me to commit to creating a life I loved living.

For the first time in my life, I put myself first. I'm not going to lie, I had trouble slowing down and quieting my mind (I still do sometimes). I didn't know what to do with my newfound freedom. It felt good being released from having to wear a suit and heels, work long hours, and travel several times a month, but I didn't know myself. I hadn't made time to dream.

I did the inner work and learned the most valuable tool: How to listen to the guidance of my Inner Voice, my Higher Self, and my Authentic Self, to create a roadmap for an authentic and fulfilling life. And I'm still on my journey but now I'm living a life I'd never imagined before.

I'm pursuing my dreams with confidence and living life on my own terms. I also help other action takers like you do the same.

I created the Onward Podcast, a weekly podcast featuring authentic conversations about facing adversity, moving forward, and discovering ourselves along the way. Then, I founded the Onward Movement which seeks to inspire you and at least 10,000 others to bravely embrace authenticity and release the fear of judgment so you can create the life of your dreams with confidence. This compassionate community is a safe place to connect and engage with others, and provides access to tools, resources, and support for each step of your journey.

## Onward Movement Roadmap

I created a roadmap for an authentic and fulfilling life based on my journey. Following this path enabled me to put myself first and create a life I absolutely love living. I'm still on my journey of self-discovery. If you're a lifelong learner like me— the journey never ends! Now I'm living a life I'd never before imagined.

The steps on the roadmap spell ONWARDER which is how we refer to Onward Movement Community members. I cover these steps when I work with my coaching clients. Here's an overview of the steps:

**Open:** Open your mind and prepare to be authentic and vulnerable as you embark upon your unique transformational journey to create the life of your dreams.

**Notice:** Notice the recurring patterns throughout your life. Become more aware and notice your beliefs about the "shoulds" in your life. Notice your longings and discontent.

**Widen:** Widen your introspection and perform an assessment of all areas your life to include: relationships, health, occupation, time and financial freedom. Also identify your top three values.

**Accept:** Learn how to remove resistance and accept your past and your present. Find the gift/opportunity in all circumstances.

**Reflect:** Reflect upon your life and all you've discovered about yourself in this coaching program. Discover and confirm your life's purpose and the legacy you want to leave.

**Dream:** Dream in all areas of your life and create your written vision for a life you've longed to love to live.

**Energize**: Be energized and more confident about creating the life of your dreams. Take daily steps toward creating a life you love living.

**Release:** Release your fear and limiting beliefs. Leave your comfort zone and you will be on your way to creating the life of your dreams. Establish a support network and share your unique story and journey with people around you and you're an Onward Movement Torchbearer.

## Mental Fitness: Building a Solid Foundation

During my transformational journey, I realized I needed to build a solid foundation to create a life I love living. Let's face it, going through the steps in the Onward Movement Roadmap can stir up some challenging thoughts and feelings. I'd always relied on physical fitness to handle stress. I've since discovered that's only part of the solution.

I wasn't mentally fit. Even though I'd retired, I felt mental stress, such as anxiety, frustration, and unhappiness, as I handled life's challenges. My hyper-achiever saboteur didn't let me enjoy retirement. I was busier than ever and I didn't know how to stop.

I decided I wanted to make improvements in this area of my life. I discovered Shirzad Chamine's New York Times bestseller, *Positive Intelligence, Why Only 20% of Teams and Individuals Achieve Their True Potential* and enrolled in his coaching program.

I learned that, we can improve our mental fitness significantly within six weeks of practice with recent breakthroughs in neuroscience and technology. I dramatically improved my performance and productivity while achieving a happier outlook, and calmer and clearer mind.

In this program, I learned about my top saboteur, my hyper-achiever. I knew I had this tendency and always thought it was a good quality. It enabled me to make it to the Senior Executive ranks in the Federal Government. Yet, I was motivated by stress and anxiety and my relationships suffered along the way.

Combining this Mental Fitness practice with my newly formed morning meditation practice significantly improved my life. I created a life I love living, a life where I'm more in flow than ever before. I'm able to choose to quiet the saboteurs in my head. I choose to not stress out over what I can't control. I more easily push away self-doubts. I run my brain rather than letting my brain run me. I was so transformed by this practice that I've incorporated Mental Fitness coaching into my offerings.

## A Final Heartfelt Thought

Becoming self-aware and mentally fit are key aspects of my transformational journey. I'd love to empower you to stop letting fear and judgment hold you back from putting yourself first, embracing authenticity, and living the life of your dreams. Join me and the Onward Movement. Let's become part of something bigger than ourselves. We're not alone – we're connected.

I know the value of this Roadmap. I've been through it and I want to help you. **I created a special webpage at www.EmilyHarman.com/Spotlight-Resources/ where you can grab a free copy of my Values Setting Workbook and the Roadmap.** We cover values setting in the Widen step of the Roadmap. Your values influence what you do, how you think, and how you feel about the world around you. Making decisions aligned to your values is key to putting yourself first and creating a life you love living.

I know you're an action taker! Here's to taking action and creating the life of **YOUR** dreams with confidence!

# About Emily Harman

A graduate of the U.S. Naval Academy, Emily served her country for 38 years as a Naval Officer and civilian. She retired as a member of the Navy's Senior Executive Service 2019. Emily's coaching is focused on helping men and women transform their dreams into reality so they can create a life they love while achieving new heights of authentic success in their personal and professional lives.

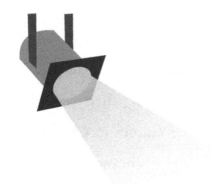

## Eve Keil

# Believe You Can and You Will

Imagine you give a performance. Afterwards, you get lots of compliments and feel like a superstar. Then you overhear some people saying you weren't that good and could have done things differently. What do you feel now? When there are two voices echoing in your head, which one do you hear? At the end of the day, what do you believe?

I grew up in China where men are leaders, and women are expected to keep their heads down and their mouths shut.

My mom was the first child born to her parents who valued boys over girls as most Chinese families do. Instead of having the most power among her younger siblings (which is supposed to be the culture in China), my mom was the one who did the household chores and took care of her siblings to prove she had value.

When I was born, I was a huge disappointment to my mom's family, and when China's one child policy started, my mom lost her only chance to add a boy to the family which meant she also lost her chance to gain respect and prove her value.

Every weekend, we would dress up to visit my mother's side of the family. The second the door opened, they would say: *"What's wrong with your hair?...Why you are dressed like a beggar?...Are you broke?"* They took every opportunity to insult us. We were only welcomed for the intense labor my mom would provide. Anything that needed to be done during the week would pile up, including a whole week's laundry for her to wash with her bare hands. Some of her siblings would throw laundry into her face and yell at her to wash it. There was **NO** respect, but my mom kept her head down and kept working while they judged her useless. But, if you think that's always how my mom acts, you're wrong! She is actually outspoken and has a bubbly personality, but whenever she was with her family, she was oftentimes shut down. Toxic relationships can change you into someone unrecognizable.

One day, I saw scars on my mom's arms and I asked her about them. She said casually, *"Oh my mom pinched me when I was a kid. I was not a good listener and talked back. It was nothing."* I felt tears inside me as I realized why she stopped speaking up and standing up for herself: she was afraid. That's the moment I knew I had to make a change. I began to talk back when I saw my mom being disrespected, but then they would attack her for being a bad mom. Eventually, I shut down too, but deep down, I never gave up. It became my mission to go to the best school, find the best job, make my mom proud, and prove to her family that she raised me well!

On my dad's side of the family, it was a totally different story. My grandma treated me like I was her world and told me how grateful she was to have me as her granddaughter. She was one of the few people who not only loved me, but also told me that out loud. She never attended school and couldn't read, but she told me powerful stories that lit fire inside me and made me feel I could move mountains. She was a true leader by setting good examples through her stories of self-determination and perseverance. In her 60's, she became Christian and she learned to read. One thing she told me over and over again was: *"Where there is a will, there is a way."*

My parents never told me they were proud of me because they didn't want me to forget to strive. They said, *"You are on your own. We don't have money, and we don't have connections. If you can't go to college, we don't have any way to find you a job. You have to work hard to earn everything for yourself."* They did encourage me to learn English for which I am forever grateful. They hoped I could one day become a translator. They never imagined I would have my own business! Instead of repeating what other people say, I have my own voice and most importantly, I empower other women to find their voices too.

So that was how I grew up with different voices in my head. I heard, *"You are worthless. You are just a girl. You just have a pretty face. That's all you got."* But I also heard, *"You are excellent! You are so smart and talented. Your potential is unlimited. You can be anything!"* So, what did I do? Who did I believe? More importantly, whom did I WANT to believe?" So, I believed I could and I did. Although I struggled with self-doubt and low self-esteem, I chose to turn up my grandma's positive voice at the back of my head.

After 12 years of hard work and dedication, I became the first person *AND* the first girl in my family to go to college. I started to make small changes in my life that may seem simple to others but ironically took me to muster courage. For example, I wore whatever style of clothes I liked. I wore-maxi dresses all winter which was uncommon in my hometown because it can sometimes get very cold. It was somewhat radical to my school back then. The director of my program wasn't a big fan of me because I was different but I didn't care. I kept being myself. I kept showing up, nevertheless. I made several good friends who loved me because of my authenticity and my confidence. That's when I realized the best outfit is confidence. As long as you are confident, you can wear any clothes or have any hair style you choose. If you believe you are beautiful the way you are, others will believe you.

Ever since I went to college, I reclaimed my freedom to be myself, and I became more confident and happier than ever. Several years later, I graduated as a top student in my class and started working for a global company in Beijing. As my life went on, I changed from married to single, from single to married again, moved from one country to another, and from a full-time professional to full-time mom. It was brutal. I was overwhelmed by self-doubt. I questioned everything including my purpose, my identity, and my self-worth. I wondered if I was a good mom or a good wife, or even loveable at all. I was back in a dark place which reminded me more of my childhood. I knew my confidence needed to be rebuilt! So, I took the first step – Show Up.

I enrolled in a Wellness Coaching Master's program and there I found my calling. I discovered my Strengths, my Purpose, my Passion and my Joy. Coaching's unique thought-provoking questioning process changed my mindset, the questions I asked myself, and my self-talk. Through coaching, I changed my own story. And from my journey, this is what I have learned:

1. **Confidence is not constant.** It changes with circumstances and must be practiced daily.
2. **We have a choice.** We can choose to believe the voice that serves us the best.
3. **We have the control.** We can't control what other people tell us but we control what we tell ourselves.

If you are ready to show up, speak up and leap into the life you deserve and desire, here is what I encourage you to do:

1. **Find your people.** Stay close with the people who love you and lift you up.
2. **Find yourself.** Find your passion, your purpose, and your strengths.
3. **Follow your passion**. You passion is your fuel!
   **Turn your pain into power.** When you remember your pain, you feel fear. But when you remember how you came through the pain, you feel strength and power.
4. **Ask for help**. Remember, you don't ask, you don't get! Nobody knows you are walking in a dark tunnel alone until you ask for help.

Empowering women is not my job; it's my passion. When I see women struggling with verbal and emotional abuse, I want to protect and defend them because I know how it feels. It reminds me of my pain which is my power today. I am using my power to change your pain into your power so you can be the most powerful and most confident version of yourself! I'm Eve Keil. Your power finder, your confidence builder. Always remember you are what you believe!

**I invite you to go to my website**

**www.EveKeil.com/spotlight-resources,**

**a special page I have just for you where I'm giving you a FREE self-affirmation guide to help you build your inner STRENGTHS and a FREE 30-minute strategy call to discuss what your strengths are and how to utilize them to succeed.** It will help you tremendously to build your confidence and find your super power. Looking forward to speaking with you!

# About Eve Keil

Eve Keil is an ICF Certified Leadership Coach and Master Coach Practitioner with two Masters in Communications and Coaching. Eve is passionate about empowering women to build their bold confidence, uncover their unique strengths, and cultivate their growth mindsets so they can live fearlessly, Love fiercely and Lead courageously. Eve has a strong track record of overcoming barriers, navigating major life transitions, and supporting C-Suits to lead, achieve and succeed.

**Jen Du Plessis**

# The Balancing Act

Do you ever feel exhausted at the end of a full day's work? Do you feel like you worked super hard, but not sure you accomplished anything? Have you done lots of activities, without real purpose or intent?

I call this "eating soup with a fork!" You come home from a long day of useless activities and feel exhausted, and not fulfilled.

So many times have we attempted to achieve the perfect "work/life balance" to achieve our full potential, the full extent of our greatness. Believing every aspect of our life must fall into "balance". I believe the opposite — that to truly live our best lives we must live our lives *out of balance*, and here's why.

If you were to look at a balanced scale, both sides would be equal, meaning 50% of your time and attention on one side, and the other 50% on the opposing side. Not 100% present or attentive to either. This means no one task or activity can get full attention to be completed efficiently or effectively. Herein lies the issue with the balancing act so many play every day.

Imagine you were straddling two boats resting in the water at one time. As the boats begin to rock back and forth, which do you pay the most attention to? If you pay attention to one, the other begins to move out of control, then you switch, but only long enough for the former to begin rocking. You are getting more tired because you are constantly task shifting from one to the other, never accomplishing balance at all.

Learning and mastering this was the key to my success in becoming a top producer in my industry. I will never forget the day I had "dinner" with my family when I received a phone call from a client. Of course, I took the call, wouldn't you? They needed me after all!

# The Balancing Act

While pacing on the concrete-balance-beam outside the restaurant, I happened to glance through the restaurant window and saw my family laughing and creating memories – except I wasn't in them! And in that moment, I knew that I had to change my ways: find a better way to achieve my goals – and find happiness. Simply making tons of money wasn't enough anymore. I wanted a way to live my life and have a killer business.

I had enough of the balancing act! I began to surrender to the myth of doing-it-all; I was present in work and at home. I cracked the code to work on purpose, spending less time working. To my delight, both my business and personal life propelled me. I never thought it was possible! All I cared about was working less and making the same money.

What I found was that my business doubled, while only working four days per week!

No more working long, unnecessary hours merely to live in daily overwhelm and chaos.

I'll be honest, it didn't come easy. It was a lot of work, years in fact, to master this beautiful skill to be able to focus every day for a short period, full of intention, and then leave to live my life. I was mastering my priorities so I could master my life.

Sure, the concept of a "balanced life" doesn't make much logical sense. So many lead a multi-dimensional life; expected to take on multiple roles, performing at the top of our game in each role we play, and the quest is virtually impossible. Success is not measured by how competently we can juggle the various aspects of our lives. Instead, it is defined by the levels of purpose, meaning and significance we invite and nurture, one at a time. *Pursuit* of our priorities automatically throws our lives out of balance – but dedicating time to our priorities, personal and professional, is a balancing act that ultimately leads to a more fulfilled life.

Discovering self-awareness, purpose, desires, and values in your personal life is essential to understanding what you need in both your personal and business lives. However, this self-awareness must be coupled with an understanding that none of these can be sacrificed for the sake of another. Equally as important, none of these can be sacrificed for your professional realm, and vice versa. Instead, they should, or could, be temporarily rearranged depending on their priority level at the time.

# The Balancing Act

Much like your personal life, managing time spent on tasks related to your professional world is crucial to your overall growth. Whether it is time spent with your friends or family, nurturing a new interest or hobby, or simply investing in quality time for yourself when focusing on professional development, it's important to remember that energy spent on your personal life can't take over that spent on your professional life. And vice versa, of course.

Improving time management is a key factor in how you effectively divide your energy between your personal and professional activities. Quality in this case is much more important than quantity – avoid viewing your tasks as items to be checked off a list and instead focus on *how* you're going to perform them. Most importantly – plan. Plan and prioritize to maximize your efficiency and organization.

For years now, I have implemented a strategy called The 12 Week Year during the first quarter of the year. This technique comes from a book of the same name written by Brian P. Moran and Michael Lennington. The concept is simple: identify your goals based on priority and create a plan to accomplish them in 12 weeks, rather than 12 months.

Without even realizing it, nearly all of us consider our goals in the context of a year. We set resolutions annually, we have one-, five- or 10-year plans. While long-term goals are good, there are problems that arise as a result. We tend to be less productive, and procrastinate more, when we think we have a deadline that's far off in the distance. This is referred to as the Parkinson's Law, which is where work expands to fill the time allotted. Ever wonder why you work so hard the last quarter of each year to reach goals you've set? Why not spread the work out throughout the year instead so that you can enjoy your life?

By making the most out of every day you will be far more likely to follow through on your responsibilities and commitments, develop and maintain your plans and have more control of your time and, ultimately, the results of your concentrated efforts.

Packing so much into a short period sounds pretty exhausting! Let me tell you, it can be at times, but it can also be exhilarating. Focusing and *doing* for such a concentrated period of time creates a genuine sense of intent and accomplishment. It also clears the path of obstacles that may have been in the way of your personal explorations and adventures. Removing critically prioritized tasks from the table makes way, and time, for personal reprieve. Working on purpose allows you to play with passion.

How do we accomplish this when we always think about what or who we aren't paying enough attention, time or energy with?

**Here are some suggestions to help.**

1.  Become ultra-clear on your business message, unique value proposition and goals. Most entrepreneurs and sales professionals wake up daily with no plan.
    Categorically know your purpose each day. Work with the intention needed to move the needle in your business and then get out of the office and go home. Stop wasting endless hours doing meaningless tasks to charm others or avoid the more meaningful work that will get you faster results.

2.  The world is always going to keep you from slowing down – you must *choose* to do so. Slowing down long enough to take a mental break, unplug, and rekindle your spirit is an essential part of your well-being – a part that far too many of us forget about. It's easy to get

caught up in throwing ourselves entirely into work and our careers, and not allowing enough time for our personal lives. Giving yourself permission to relax and recharge opens so many doors and exposes a wealth of opportunities. Use this *intermission* to explore and expand your creative side, develop new interests, or work on your existing hobbies.

**I created a thought-provoking exercise to help you begin your journey - 7 Strategies to Breakthrough your Business Mindset." You can get access to it at**

**www.JenDuPlessis.com/SpotlightResources**

It will help you assess 7 areas of your life and business to gain clarity of where you are now and where, and who, you want to be in the future.

It's time you begin to live your legacy while you're building it, rather than building it and hoping you have enough time to live it later. Be as good to yourself as you are to your business, your life will thank you!

# About Jen Du Plessis

Tell her she can't, and she will show you how she did it! You can do it too! With 38 years in leadership, sales and entrepreneurship, Jen mentors professionals how to live their legacy while building it! She is a charismatic speaker, business coach and mentor, two-time #1 Best Selling Author of LAUNCH! and IMPACT, TV Show host and 2-show Podcaster.

**Katrina Sawa**

# Becoming An
# Online Authority

One essential part of being a successful entrepreneur these days is how you "show up" in your industry and what you look like to your potential prospects. This is called your *Online Authority*.

Whether you enjoy being a leader in your industry, you crave the spotlight with what you're doing or you're someone who wants to fly under the radar in your life and lay low; it's important to build your Online Authority. Your Online Authority is your digital presence or digital footprint.

**Why is it important to be an *Online Authority* rather than just an *Authority* which many people suggest?** It's different.

Being an Online Authority is compiled of the following:

- Website
- Branding
- Messaging
- Image
- Confidence
- Social presence and following
- On camera personality
- Photos
- Digital footprint

Regardless of what type of company or business you might be building, these things now need to be foundational pieces of your business pie. Everything you're doing, everywhere online and offline have to flow together to form this Online Authority Image for yourself.

## Definition of authority: power to influence or command thought, opinion, or behavior

Being an Authority to those of us in the entrepreneurial space used to mean that you were someone that is looked up to or that has a large following. It can also mean someone who is a leader. But an Online Authority takes it one step further whereas you have to "look the part" as well.

What do you "look like" to the outside world?

- Do you look credible?
- Are you trustworthy?
- Is it believable that you know what you're doing or have the expertise you claim to have?
- Are you well known?
- Are others talking about you?
- Do you share relevant content?
- Does your information seem fresh or unique?
- Do you look financially successful?
- Are you walking your talk?
- Are you believable?
- Are you being vulnerable and letting people in?
- Do you have a cohesive brand message?

- And do you look like this in every corner of the digital world?

So, are you looking at this list frightened to death because you're afraid of putting yourself out there in such a big way?

Or are you thinking to yourself: "Does this all matter? Come on, there must be an easier way?"

Or maybe you think you have all this covered already and "you're good"; yet you're not seeing the financial results you'd hoped you would see by now?

Well, as a business coach since 2002, I can tell you that these all DO matter NOW. It didn't matter back when I started, but it does now.

And while I've not had a hard time stepping into the spotlight or putting myself out there more, I secretly love that part, I still have my moments of doubt, fear and sometimes even some Imposter Syndrome. This is all very common, and you wouldn't be human if you didn't have a part of you who doubted your abilities on some level.

It's what you DO about it now knowing this that will make or break your success!

You see, my love for the spotlight came from my time as a little girl, being an only child for the first 10 years of my life, I craved attention all the time.

For me, I felt very alone. At times I either had a dog or a cat or maybe both to play with but it still wasn't enough. I remember pulling out board games from the closet and laying them out on my bedroom floor, getting up and physically moving myself from one side of the board game to the other until I would play each players' turn in the game. The good part was I always won! The bad part, of course, was a constant longing for someone to play with.

I don't really recall in those first ten years how often my parents would actually play with me. I know at age 5 they got divorced. The divorce made it even worse because that means I only had one of their attention at any given point. I lived with my mom the majority of the time except for maybe one or two weeks during the summer when I would go visit my dad wherever he was living (he moved around a lot). When she started dating again, she had even less time for me. By no means was she a bad mom, there just wasn't enough time for me, as I can recall.

I remember getting in trouble in fourth grade with the police because I was doing something I shouldn't be; again, trying to get attention. It wasn't anything too serious and it didn't give me a record or anything, it just scared the heck out of me which was probably a good thing to keep me in line.

I remember another time kneeling backwards on the couch of our two-bedroom condo looking out the front window with anticipation because my Dad was supposed to come pick me up that day. He never showed up that day or the day after and I was devastated. When he finally did show up he made some excuse that I didn't even recall. This made me feel really unloved and unworthy which festered in my subconscious for the next 35 years.

Looking back on my childhood, now at age 51, I can see why I always wanted to be in the spotlight, as an adult and all through high school and college, it makes sense. I was Co-Captain of the dance squad as a senior and, along with 16 of my friends in college, we started our own sorority where I became the Social Chair, the spotlight was my drug of choice.

As a business owner, being in the spotlight to me means shining on stage, in person or even virtual stages and events. I love speaking and events. I do both to attract clients and educate or inspire the entrepreneurs I work with. It means getting on television with free publicity, which I've been able to do almost a dozen times so far.

Being in the spotlight even means elevating myself into a real Online Authority too. As I mentioned, this is one of the most essential parts of being a successful and profitable entrepreneur. You have to "look the part". The people who make a lot of money have great exposure, branding and marketing; they look great online.

Those who don't "look the part" just don't seem to do as well. Why is that?

People want to model after and follow successful-looking people. They tend to trust successful- looking people more than unsuccessful-looking people. And if you have an online presence, brand, and positioning that isn't very exciting, up-to-date, and impressive, then you'll lose the business to the person who "looks the part" better than you.

And frankly, having great positioning, branding and a really impressive online presence doesn't have to cost a mint like you might believe. But you have to pay a lot more attention to this than ever before.

Regardless of what type of company or business you might be building, these things now need to be foundational pieces that you get expert advice and strategy around from the start. And if you're not seeing very good results and you've been in business for 2, 3, or even 5 years, then it could be that you never really focused on these things in the beginning, or it didn't matter as much as it does now. Now, you are seeing your business stagnate and you aren't sure why. It's very possible that it has to do with your lack of Online Authority.

So, what can you do about enhancing your Online Authority today?

That's where I come in and possibly other experts in this book as well. As a business and marketing coach, publishing expert and speaker trainer, I can help you in all areas of building your Online Authority, positioning you as the most sought-after expert in your field and show you how to monetize it all a whole heck of a lot more too!

**I put together a special page on my website at www.JumpstartYourAuthority.com where I'm going to give you Free Access to a few of my trainings just for reading this chapter.** When you sign up over there, you'll receive my:

- **Jumpstart Yourself as a Speaker Audio Training**

- **Jumpstart Yourself as an Author Publishing Info Call**

- **Jumpstart Your Marketing Basics 3-Part Webinar Training**

- **And an opportunity to have a Free Coaching Call with me!**

You can do this - I can help!

Doing what you have always done will result in what you have always received. You have to take the steps necessary to get to where you want to go. You can get there faster with bigger leaps of faith or you can get there slower with baby steps. It's up to you but get started today - a better life and more profitable business is waiting for you!

# About Katrina Sawa

The JumpStart Your Biz Coach, Katrina Sawa, is the creator of the JumpStart Your Marketing & Sales Systems, a tell-it-like-it-is speaker, and a 7x International Best-Selling author with 11 books. She is the CEO of JumpstartYourBizNow.com and JumpstartPublishing.net. Katrina has a no-nonsense approach to developing consistently profitable businesses implementing proven marketing and business strategies. She's been featured on the Oprah and Friends XMRadioNetwork, ABC, TheCW and dozens of influential podcasts.

### Dr. Laura Cobb

---

# Step Into Your Why

You deserve an abundant life full of love, happiness, and fulfillment. You might wonder how I could possibly know that since I don't know you. What I do know, is that you are reading this particular chapter in this specific book. This means you desired something, you moved in the direction to fulfill that craving, and are following through with action in order to meet a goal.

The question then begs: What is a goal and what is the action we take to obtain it?

Consider this: Three frogs sit on a log. Two decide to jump off. How many are left?

Three.

Why? Because a purpose without conscious movement is an unfulfilled dream.

You may have 100% pure intention of obtaining a goal. However, such motives must involve action to create behavioral shifts. Overtime, these shifts change the beliefs we have and thus, we become empowered to create a purposeful life.

I've cultivated a purpose-driven life over the course of more than four decades. Sure, I've set goals. Yet, it's the actions I take that increase the likelihood of success. The challenge becomes identifying the desire, the why, to move in the direction of obtaining the goal and the effort put forth to achieve it. Said in a similar way, *'what do you want, why do you want it, and to what lengths are you willing to work for it?'*

What do you want?

The "what" in a purpose-driven, abundant life depends on what is meaningful in that moment. For example, although I was encouraged to skip 1st and 2nd grades, I wasn't interested. My friends at school provided respite from my overbearing siblings who habitually bullied me. What I wanted was to feel safe, which school provided.

Everything changed when I started college. I love it and I was good at it. My journey was a relentless determination to succeed, pushing myself so that eventually I did make it to the top. I was unbeatable and I became comfortable with that level of success. It was so easy that during the final year of my doctorate, while writing my dissertation, I got married, moved to Germany, and started a second master's degree.

Almost twelve years later, I walked across the graduation stage and looked over my shoulder as the dean said, "Congratulations Dr. Cobb." The name seemed foreign and meant for someone else. Realizing she was talking to me, I continued to my seat. It felt wonderful with the knowledge that I'd earned this title. So good for about fifteen seconds. Yes, fifteen seconds of my heart racing and my adrenaline pumping. Fifteen seconds of, "Yeah, I did it!" Fifteen seconds of euphoria.

On the sixteenth second, I looked around at all of the other "doctors" and I thought, that's it? What just happened? Where are the balloons? The parade? I thought all of my problems would fade away in comparison to this amazing achievement. None of that happened. Not even in my heart. I felt nothing. I was shocked.

What's your why?

Why would anyone spend twelve years in college? Why would anyone start a second master's degree while writing a dissertation while getting married and moving overseas? Did I truly enjoy school?

I questioned myself for quite some time until years later, after a mid-life breakdown forced me to slow down. I realized that I was afraid to grow up and become an adult. What better way to extend my adolescence than to stay in school? Not only was I recognized for it, but I was applauded.

My family was proud of me... as was I. I felt valued with the praise for the exemplary grades, the scholarships, and the subsequent degrees I earned. This carried over into my professional career as well—the promotions, accolades, and the prestige. What no one knew, not even me, was why I was so driven to achieve such almost-unobtainable accomplishments.

My why is an acronym for:

Who

Hears

You

Toni Morrison once said, *"When your child walks into the room, do your eyes light up?"*

I didn't experience that as a child. I didn't feel seen or heard except as "the baby." I had a brother who was the life of the party, another who was awkward and socially inept, and a sister who was a prom queen and cheerleader. I felt invisible growing up. I wanted someone to know that I wasn't happy.

I didn't understand no one intervened when I described the hurt from being bullied. I wondered if anyone thought about me as I was grounded for an entire summer after changing a grade on my 3rd grade report card. Sometimes my feelings were so strong they scared me. I wondered if my parents heard me crying in my bedroom. I longed for my stepdad to speak to me and my father to acknowledge me when they found out that I'd discovered boys. So, my role as "scholar" was born as my family responded with praise and pride for my efforts. I was seen.

I consider every experience, every encounter, and particularly every mistake is presented to force us into being more of who we are. Our job is to figure out what is the next right move. The key to life is to develop an internal moral and emotional compass to guide us in the direction of our purpose. Our job is to follow our purpose and to live an abundant life.

What are you willing to do?

The effort to achieve a goal is admirable, but it should not be done for the sole purpose of a goal's sake at the expense of connection with others. Looking back, I realize that the stress of my pursuits and my name said out loud was paid for with the lack of attending to relationships. I chose those pursuits at the detriment of my loved ones. I was a thief. I stole precious time for perceived status.

I believed that being busy was a sign of being productive, and it was, for a while. At the same time, I was lonelier than I'd ever been. Each additional degree, award, scholarship, and accolade I achieved culminated in a fleeting sense of satisfaction and self-worth, only to fade into setting the bar higher for myself. It felt like an achiever's curse.

Logically, while constantly raising the bar and constantly pushing higher, the law of averages predicts that failure must occur at some point. When that happens, always remember that failure doesn't mean losing. What goes up must come down. Failure stops us from continuing in the same pattern--

for a moment. The pivotal point is that once we fall, we have to be willing to do what we need to do to rise up.

The moment everything changed for me was when I realized I deserved so much more than what I was giving to myself and what I was allowing others to do to me. I went through some tough times that led me to being homeless for a short time, without my son even, and I climbed out of that with more purpose than ever.

For the better part of the last ten years, I had to spoon-feed myself those words. I allowed myself to feel low for a little while. The key is to learn from what's happened. Every experience, every encounter and every mistake, you are forced into being more of who you are and then figure out what is the next right move. Another key to life is to develop an internal moral and emotional compass that can tell you which way to go.

The challenge of life is to build a resume that doesn't simply tell a story about what you accomplished or what you hope to achieve. It's not a collection of titles and positions. Your life is a story that's focused on your purpose. Because when you inevitably stumble and find yourself stuck in a hole, your story will lead you out. When you find yourself in that place, ask yourself three questions:

1. What do you want to do?
2. Why do you want what you want?
3. How much are you willing to work to achieve what you want?

Here's the lesson: have no regrets in the sixteenth second. Nothing is more important than your healthy relationships— nothing, not your goals, not your successes. Here's how I understand the W.H.Y. Relationships are where we get to influence, impact, and change people's lives. Your life cannot be meaningful without them. We all have a purpose to advance. How we go about that is what's different. It's different in what college we choose, who we marry, and what career we choose. It's different in the triumphs and tragedies that come upon us. Yet, in all those things, new relationships are formed as you live your life on this earth. There is no greater good you can do for a person than to love them so much that you serve as a light to follow so they can find the shore when they are lost.

Make sure you care for that relationship above all others. After that, prioritize what is important and never lose focus. Be generous with your time and a lot of relational issues will be resolved. It's never too late to mend fractured relationships. Humble yourself to start a conversation so that you have no regrets in the sixteenth second.

I invite you to download a free copy of an eBook on my website called: *Step Into Your WHY* where you will enjoy e-Book "Make Your Life More Fulfilling and Discover Your Life Purpose. Go to www.DrLauraCobbLifeCoach.com/SpotlightBookReso urces today and get access.

# About Dr. Laura Cobb
# PhD., LPC

Dr. Laura Cobb, Ph.D. is an Empowerment Coach and Nationally Certified and Licensed Professional Counselor. She inspires ambitious, successful, professional women to live confident, authentic lives. Dr. Cobb specializes in family life education, resilience, mindset training, and mental fitness. She is a subject matter expert on mental and emotional health, addiction and abuse, sexual assault, imposter syndrome and career-related content.

Theresa Sperling

# Embracing Public Speaking To Grow Your Influence

Ever since I was a child, I was a master at avoiding the spotlight. I had some remarkable strategies to avoid being called on in class. My best moves were:

*To keep my head up and furrow my brow like I was still thinking;*

*Tell the instructor that I was still working on the problem; or*

*As an adult student: ask a question back to the instructor;*

A state that I didn't understand an aspect of what was before me, or

*I would like more time or information to form a solid opinion.*

I was content to closely observe any situation, keeping my ideas and opinions to myself. After all, who wants to hear what I have to say anyway? And, why should I just give away my ideas? That second question always made me feel better and satisfied that I knew the truth. My ideas were fantastic, and they would remain with me.

After many years of riding a roller coaster career, I landed a dream position as a corporate trainer. My main responsibility would be to conduct classroom training. The offer was so good; I accepted the position on the spot. Driving home, I began to realize what I had just agreed to do. I would now spend most of my time in front of a group of people, staring at me and depending on me, to teach them the skills they needed to be successful. The panic set in.

I wanted this job and I wanted to be successful at it. This became a turning point in my life. I decided I would become the best trainer and speaker possible. I told myself, *"YES! I could get up in front of people and speak"*. Failure was not an option.

As we all know, public speaking is the major fear for most people. I, however, wanted to join the small number of people who could do it and not only survive the whole experience, but be amazing at it.

Since then, I have become a bit of a public speaking groupie. I seek out speakers and topics that I want to know more about. It has become more of a full sensory experience for me. I receive a speaker's message in layers like: *What am I hearing? What am I seeing? What am I feeling?* This unique way of experiencing speakers has led me to train and mentor others to effectively deliver their message so that they get their desired results.

Public speaking is an incredible tool to market your business or non-profit organization. It is the fastest path to more clients, more donors, or more awareness, which all lead to more cash in your pocket. The catch is that you need to be well trained as a speaker to walk on that quick path to results.

We have all heard a million times that people do business with people they know, like, and trust. Speaking to promote and grow your business accelerates those *know, like, and trust* factors. When you are the speaker, there is a built-in credibility as the expert. This is your foundation of the trust factor.

The audience is warm versus picking up the telephone for a cold call. Audience members either know you are the speaker or know the topic you will share. Thus, there is an interest and a pool of potential clients ready to hear your message. This is your foundation of the know factor.

As the speaker, you will need to bring several more factors to your talk. Most importantly, you will need to be likeable to win over potential clients. Speaking is your opportunity to showcase yourself. It also gives the audience a significant timeframe to decide just how much they like you.

Traditional marketing efforts typically take seven touches to get a potential client to even pay attention to your message. With more and more pieces of information competing for our time and attention, it is now more along the lines of 17 touches to get a potential client to receive your message. Since speaking can save you time and effort to get someone to listen to your message, plus you capture their time and attention, it is truly one of the best-kept secrets for marketing your business or organization.

**Here are my Three Secrets to help you Step into the Speaking Spotlight:**

## 1. Improve your public speaking skills.

It is important to grasp the concept that public speaking is a valuable marketing tool. It is also a learned skill. This means anyone, and I mean anyone, can speak in front of people and, with practice, can create an outstanding audience experience.

I mentioned earlier some reasons why you should implement public speaking into your marketing efforts. Speaking to groups is a highly effective way to share your message and leverage your time. It is an opportunity, when done well, which allows you to showcase your expertise and win new clients. Remember, it is the fastest path to cash.

Would you rather make multiple cold calls? Or, speak to a warm audience? Again, the audience, in most cases, will have a bit of an idea on what you will be saying and what you are going to talk about. If they don't want to hear it, they are free to leave. But most will not leave once you have started talking. I teach my clients to repeat to themselves, "They want to hear what I have to say".

Who cares if it is true? You just need to believe it while you are in the spotlight. Can you do that for five, ten, or 20 minutes? This leads to my second secret.

## 2. Use positive self-talk and visualization.

As stated above, believe the audience is there to hear your message. Further, believe that you will be successful on stage. You can truly become an impactful speaker by practicing your talk over and over. I am not advising you to memorize your talk. Practice it until it flows as a natural story that you share with audiences.

Visualize your speech going well, your audience reacting positively, and audience members waiting to talk with you afterwards. A quick note about your audience: there may not be many smiling or friendly looking faces. It is not a direct response to you. When people concentrate on what you are saying, they may have a more serious facial expression. Try to find a person with a softer expression to look at occasionally if you feel you are getting nervous.

## 3. Use nervousness to your advantage.

Whenever I tell someone what I do, the most common response is, "Oh, I could never do that. I would be too nervous." First of all, it is ok to be nervous. You just need to learn how to control the outward signs of nervousness. You may be surprised to learn that many seasoned speakers still get nervous before taking the stage. They, however, have figured out how to use nervousness to their advantage.

Did you know that the physical symptoms of an athlete's adrenaline and a presenter's nervousness are precisely the same? The only difference is how the brain interprets the feeling. Established speakers know how to channel their nervousness into excitement to step into the spotlight. They recognize their specific signs or expressions of nervousness and have practiced ways to control them. In fact, seasoned speakers have turned that nervousness into the equivalent of a runner's high. They thrive on that feeling and use it to bring enthusiasm to the stage. Audiences love enthusiasm.

Overcoming expressions of nervousness can be a major obstacle. It will take time to recognize what exactly you do and how to control it. This is a crucial step in improving your speaking skills, as these expressions can turn into huge distractions for your audience.

To help you become more familiar with the most common audience distractions, I have created a valuable resource called, *"The Dirty Dozen Distractions"*. **This is a complimentary gift to readers of this book. Please visit my website to request your free electronic copy of "The Dirty Dozen Distractions":**

**www.TheresaSperling.com/spotlightresource**

By using my secrets above, you can say yes to opportunities to speak and grow your business. No more stressing out. No more missing out on speaking opportunities. And, no more feeling like you have failed.

I challenge you to change your thinking about speaking publicly from something negative or problematic into a useful marketing tool that contributes to your bottom line. It is a skill you can learn or improve upon.

As an introvert, I now enjoy speaking and the spotlight. Yes, I have crashed and burned. Yes, I have embarrassed myself. But I survived. I have joined the "Survivors Club of Public Speaking". I see so many members are doing brilliant things to change the world and I am glad to be here. I invite you to join us. I will be waiting for you in the wonderful warmth of the spotlight.

# About Theresa Sperling

Theresa Sperling has an extensive background in training and mentoring, specifically in speaking and leadership. She thoroughly enjoys working with clients to help them gain the confidence to share their message and get results. She has worked with beginners to international speakers who have sought her feedback. Theresa is a member of Toastmasters and Rotary, an elected community leader, and a loving dog mom.

Tricia Parido

# How Living Life Without Habits Fixes Everything

You might be a little confused by this title and what could I mean by living life without habits.-Habits are amazing and they keep us productive, profitable, and focused.

Yet what I'm really talking about are the habits that we don't want to keep, the addictive ones that get in the way of managing our life, our business, family and our own affairs.

115

I'm Tricia Parido, a Recovery Lifestyle Speaker, Personal Life Coach, Master Addictions Specialist, wife, mother, grandmother...

I'm a fierce optimist who is dedicated to helping you change your life! My passion is to help you dream again, collaborate a plan for you, and equip you with skills and tools to attain it! I know how challenging it can be to create a healthy lifestyle, especially one that's fulfilling. After 30 years of trauma, loss, assaults, violence, addiction, eating disorders, body dysmorphia, a lacking sense of self, severe anxiety and everything that comes with that path, I finally arrived where I am *today*. Living Life, living it freely, without feeling guilty, selfish, punished, or restricted! And it's all because of my support and the steps I took to make sure I got to live my life the way I saw fit!

My chemical dependence alone spanned 30 years of my life and my recovery journey has been 25+ years. There wasn't a specific model that met all of my needs and all of my needs weren't ready to be healed at the same time. You see the deeper I got into my recovery process the more I uncovered. In fact, I took the time while getting my degree to not only study addiction treatment, I studied the psychology of addiction in greater depth; process, behavioral, and chemical in nature, uncovering issues such as impulsive shopping, people pleasing codependency, and perfectionism. This is where I discovered the *Locus of Control theory*.

During this 5 ½ years of psychological journey with myself as the case study I also submerged myself on the clinical side of every level of addiction treatment/care that was made available. What I discovered about myself and every client that I had the pleasure to work with thereafter was that there was this driving force— a force that was overwhelming, scary, frustrating, irritating, devastating and very much anxiety inducing that consistently derailed any coping mechanisms, and left me feeling out of control.

This force drove me to negative reactivity, to cover up the uncomfortable, hide from the unbearable, elevate my demeanor, give me a bravado that would push me through, even calm me enough to just breathe.

That drive that said bad things always happen to me, the world is scary, people are cruel; *"You can do better"*, *"You can be better"*, *"They don't like me"*, *"They think I'm stupid"*, *"They are out to get me"*, *"Everyone leaves me"*.

People struggling with addiction or who are being held hostage by their habits and negative attachments need to understand that they get to choose how they experience their environment.

Taking control of my thoughts, feelings, emotions, opinion and beliefs did not come simply because I learned this particular theory!

It was absolutely one of the most significant lessons I have learned in life.

But I had to dig in and compile a gamete of skill sets and tactics that would generate the strength and capability necessary to make living through my internal drive a lifelong manageable and maintaining attainment!

So, let's bring in some relatability.

- Have you ever overindulged in food? Maybe you have a tendency to buy yourself a treat and eat it in the car so nobody knows?

- How about your shopping habits? Do you hide things you buy?

- Can you picture yourself making an excuse to go to the kitchen just so you can secretly top off your glass of wine? Maybe you don't want anybody to know how fast you are really drinking? While everybody else is off at work or school do you have a couple drinks while vacuuming or some other chore?

I think we all have at least one secret indulgence and maybe some of us are tormented by them more than others. All of these methods for coping just bring more grief.

When I got to the place in my life where I had just had enough - I was tired of trying to find that right time for a beer - I was tired of restricting myself after bingeing on ice cream or cookies - I was ever so tired of trying to justify my unnecessary purchases - I was just tired of it all.

There was a lot of observing, learning, researching, practicing, restructuring, and implementing on my journey. What it all boiled down to is eight very significant processes and ways of functioning.

## 8 Steps to Live Life WITHOUT Habits

1. **You must genuinely know yourself!** Every piece that makes your Emotional, intellectual, physical, social, environmental, and spiritual being function. That internal dialogue and personal evaluation of your worthiness, value, validity, genuineness, self-love, honor

and respect must be congruent with how you want to see yourself, which takes operating from an intuitive mindset – one that balances out that emotional reactivity and the rationalizations. Which also means you have to ditch your pressure filled should statements!

2. **You must adjust how you're functioning! Balance goes far deeper than between home and work.** I focus on eight primary categories and the piece that represents health has six subcategories. You also can't go with definitions based on a book or someone else's assessment of what belongs in them. You must define their meaning for you and for you alone. And to keep things running smoothly it's important that you can become centered and grounded in ANY moment. In those times where meditation and dropping into a yoga pose just aren't feasible. This takes personal investigation, an effective tool kit and conditioning.

3. **You must abandon your reactivity – that knee jerk instantaneous system that has been embedded in your functioning.** You must become responsive in all actions. And to do this, you must cultivate the art of pause.

4. **You need to clearly understand what drive you operate from internal or external.** If things outside of you have the power to change your mood, actions, and so on, you should have a functional internal control system. Then you will need to get assertive with your thoughts, feelings, emotions, options, beliefs, needs and wants. No more wishy-washy passive aggressiveness.

5. **You need a filtrating boundary system that is backed by healthy limits and limitations to protect yourself.** There are four boundaries that keep you safe and protect the ones you love as well: Internal, External, Temporal, and Physical. The limits and limitations are the hard-fast stops.

6. **You must shift into being effective and doing what works.** This means being mindful and willing to evaluate how you handle yourself. Investigate how you hear. Develop the capacity to move into resolution and cultivate tactics of assertiveness that will serve every piece of your life and the relationships within it.

7. **You must learn to control your moments – especially in times of distress.** This means learning what self-soothing looks like, having effective

121

distractions handy, and knowing YOUR secret that will improve your experiences.

8. **You must Leave the pain behind and lead with a new lens**. It's time to identify and describe our emotions. Better yet how to observe and visualize letting them go. There is a way for each of us to regulate emotions and reduce vulnerability. Realize that wallowing and ruminating don't serve us. All we have is the here and now. Yesterday has passed – we clearly survived it – tomorrow hasn't arrived – we can't control it – but what we do today will be our foundation.

It's time for you to shine! I am going to leave you with three final rules that will change your life, change how you utilize the things you gain inside this book, allow you to move through all life transitions effectively and with resilience, even in the face of adversity. (1) Add (2) Edit and (3) Delete!

You have taken the time to put yourself in a position to learn something useful and to help you improve your life so make the most of it! Don't try to make your life fit into a practice or method! Instead integrate the method or the practice effectively into your life and in a fashion that will accentuate the unique individual being you are.

Remember, personal drive is a combination of desire and energy in its simplest form directed at achieving a goal in whatever you have set your heart to accomplish.

**If you are motivated to create your mastery and you want more information from me, I would love to offer you access to my 3-Part Series "Turning a New Leaf" that will get you started! Just go to**

**www.TriciaParido.com/giveaway**
**now where I'm giving this to you as my gift.**

# About Tricia Parido

**BS Psych, IMAC, NCPLC, CATCIII, NCIP, NCPCM**

Tricia Parido is a Recovery Lifestyle Enthusiast, Speaker, and Writer. She is a Nationally Certified Life Coach, an International Master Addictions Specialist and a Professional Life Interventionist with a Psych Degree in Process Behavioral and Chemical Addiction who loves to help change lives! Specializing in life transitions and post-treatment journeys, Parido is ever committed to serving her clients worldwide find the emotional intelligence they need to conquer their life challenges.

## Colleen Biggs

# What's Next?

**What did you think of the stories and expertise that our authors had to share?**

**Did you learn a few new things to take back to your life or work?**

My hope is that you did learn a few things, or at least walk away with a fresh new way of thinking. If so, please go over to Amazon and leave us a review! Reviews assist the next individual in making the decisions on whether they believe this book will impact their lives. If it impacted yours, tell us about it!

Our authors have been hand-selected based on their level of expertise, genuine integrity, and overall skill level in their industry. If you enjoyed reading some of their stories or learning more about them, please take the next step and reach out to those who spoke to you. You can find their contact information within each of their chapters or you can also go check out some additional in-depth interviews of our Authors here, along with some additional freebies from each one. www.StepIntoTheSpotlightResources.com

Most of the authors in this book speak to groups of all sizes, both in person and virtually. They also offer products, programs, events, and services that can support you in one or more areas of your life, health, or business / career.

I highly recommend that you take advantage of their special offers, additional downloads, and more when you visit each of the websites listed at the end of their chapters.

Get to know the 11 Motivated Authors in this book!

Getting to know the authors and adding the additional benefit to dive deeper into their stories and strategies is available to you anytime, anywhere.

Go to www.StepIntoTheSpotlightResources.com now before you forget for private video interviews with each author. Bookmark the page and forever return for inspiring messages, reminders of how to expand our influence, and consistent practices to apply to your business and life today. For a list of the authors, turn to the table of contents page.

As a Corporate dropout turned millionaire in 3 years of showing up and stepping into the spotlight in the entrepreneurial world I call the "Millionaire Playground", I believe we all have the opportunity to create the lives of our dreams by stepping into the spotlight! If you would like to know more about how to become an author in one of our next books, visit me at www.ColleenBiggs.net.

If you'd like to join a community of strong women doing big things, then head over to

www.ColleenBiggs.net/community

and join us! Tomorrow is not promised and today will turn into yesterday. When is the right time for you to expand your influence? The time is NOW!

Thank you for reading this book, and I look forward to bringing you more Authors in upcoming books, plus more training and teachings in my own books.

## About Colleen Biggs

# CEO & Founder, B You B Strong LLC.

Colleen Biggs is an Award-Winning Leadership Coach that empowers successful women leaders to create a bigger impact by leaning into their fullest purpose to reach their peak potential so they can inspire change in others, build unlimited success, and leave a legacy behind. She has extensive success and experience in Corporate America for over 30 years, consulting over 340 business start-ups, franchising, and voluntary national and local community service.

She is an author of 5 #1 Best-Selling International Books, with *Step into the spotlight* being the 5th. She is an elite podcast host, and interviews powerful leaders to inspire, educate, and motivate on how they took the leap in business and their lives. Take the Leap with Colleen Biggs can be found on Apple here:

https://tinyurl.com/yckn6be4

She has also published two Journals on Amazon here:

https://tinyurl.com/bdfnp27v

Colleen built the Lead Up for Women Community from 2018 through 2021 to over 10,000 women and is now the CEO and Founder of L.E.A.P. She was recently awarded the 2020 Local person of the year and 2021 awarded Top 10 Businesswomen. Colleen provides women with a community of entrepreneurs that take the leap daily and realize that their network is their net worth.

Colleen and her husband Robert are happily married, living in Mesa, AZ with 7 beautiful children and 12 VERY busy grandchildren. Colleen and Robert enjoy traditions and have created several in their lives. Every Christmas each one of the family members receives an ornament for the greatest accomplishment achieved that year. They also host regular monthly pizza nights that include each person making their own personal pizza while playing games and taking the grandkids on treasure hunts.

**66**

*You are the only you that has ever been, and the only you that will ever be, you are one of a kind.*

- Colleen Biggs

# SPOTLIGHT
# RESOURCES

# Motivate and Inspire Others!
## *"Share this Book"*

**Retail $14.95 + Tax & Shipping**

**Special Quantity Discounts**

| | |
|---|---|
| **5 - 15 Books** | **$11.95 Each** |
| **16 - 30 Books** | **$9.95 Each** |
| **30 - 1,000 Books** | **$7.95 Each** |

**To Place an Order Contact:**
Colleen Biggs | B You B Strong, LLC
**(602) 730-5121**
**info@colleenbiggs.net**
Or go to ColleenBiggs.net

# Want to Become an Author or Learn how to Publish a Book?

Professional Book Writing and publishing is Easy if you know WHAT to do, WHERE to get stuff done, and HOW to publish, especially if you want to do it the most affordable way possible, yet still have a very professional looking book.

**Do You Have a Draft, or an Idea for a Book but Don't Know How to Get It Done & Turn It Into a Real Print Book?**

**You may need:**

- Support to finish and fine tune the manuscript

- A beautifully designed cover

- A great editor to make your book sing

- A marketing plan for book launch and sales

- A book webpage or author website

- And so much more…

**Access a free training and info about publishing and becoming an author today, don't wait! Go to www.JumpstartPublishing.net.**

# Book Colleen to Speak:

Colleen Biggs is an International, Inspirational Speaker. The topics of her presentations include:

- *Step in the Spotlight to Expand Your Influence*
- *Community Fosters Strong Female Leadership*
- *Master You to Master Your Success*

*"Colleen Biggs is heading a movement. She is empowering women to reach their full potential. She has proven to be an exceptional leader at a time when people need innovation direction. She provides exceptional content through her Facebook live posts, Teaching Tuesdays, Thrive Thursdays, and podcast programs. Her semi-monthly magazine Lead Up for Women showcases important topics for business owners."*
*– Debi C.*

**Contact Colleen to Speak Today!**
B You B Strong, LLC
(480) 241-3708 | info@colleenbiggs.net
ColleenBiggs.net

# Are you tired of the overcrowded social media platforms? Me too!

## *Join the Leap Community!*

The Leap Community will showcase you in ways that will allow you to BE SEEN, BE HEARD, and BE VISIBLE. The #1 rule in a business building that I have taught over 340 CEO's to build successful businesses is *"Tell everyone about YOU"*.

Visit us at

www.colleenbiggs.net/community

**Here are just a few of the Members Perks that are included with your Leap membership:**

- Interview Opportunity to be a **guest on the Podcast** to promote you, your story/message, and business
- Weekly Book Club for **Personal Development**
- **Live LinkedIn Interviews** through our Member Monday Spotlight to promote you, your story/message, and business
- Exclusive access to our online Blog posts and the **ability to contribute as a member** for maximum visibility for your brand and message.
- **Host a #Thrive Thursday Masterclass** that will promote you, your company, and your message and many may more opportunities.

To learn more about all the membership perks and how you can join this community of like-minded females, visit us at

www.colleenbiggs.net/community

We can't wait to meet you!

Download 7 ways to quick visibility and start expanding your influence today!

www.colleenbiggs.net/freebies

LEAD with
ENHANCED ACCELERATION
to reach your
PEAK PERFORMANCE

# Are you ready to take the L.E.A.P.?

Colleen Biggs has extensive success and experience for over 20 years consulting over 340 business launches. It's because she starts with providing her clients a strategic approach to using their experience, wisdom, strengths, and skillsets to build and scale a successful, profitable business. Colleen offers several levels of professional business and leadership coaching.

Colleen was awarded Local Businessperson of the year in 2020 and 2021 top 10 Business Leaders. Colleen leads successful businesses, 2 of those businesses reaching over $100,000 within the first 2 months. She could not achieve these levels of success without a strategic business plan (Acceleration blueprint), Community, increased productivity through time-blocking, and her invincible attitude!

# Why Work with Colleen?

Wouldn't it be great if you had the clarity to see beyond your blind spots?

Wouldn't it be great to know exactly what sets you apart and to know what to say to leave a lasting impression?

Being confident in what you offer and what sets you apart from your competition is only the beginning. Armed with the right tools, clarity, community, UNSTOPPABLE STRENGTH and strategic plan makes increasing revenue a breeze! I think we can all agree that with this combination, your business, would be more profitable and you would spend the hours in your day doing what you love!

# What's in It for Me?

I'm so glad you asked because this is all about YOU and YOUR business

Here's what you can expect to gain:

- Increased clarity of your current offering and where you are leaving money on the table, then we go to work!
- A community and tribe of women that will support and lift you
- A fresh perspective on fun and excitement in your business
- Increased strength in the belief of your unique power and what sets you apart from others
- How to attract your ideal client and the steps to make it happen
- Gain an invincible attitude, not to be confused with ego, those don't reside here!
- Steps to achieving the success in your business you desire as we work towards your persona goals
- Unshakeable Confidence!!

**To learn more about your options and how you can take the L.E.A.P. your business deserves, visit ColleenBiggs.net.**

**66**

*Your true potential will speak as loud as your willingness to listen will allow it.*

- Mary Morrissey

# 66

*If you do what is easy your life will be hard, if you do it as hard your life will be easy.*

- Les Brown

**99**